THE COMPASSION BOOK

D0957093

Also by Pema Chödrön

THE COMPASSION BOOK
Teachings for Awakening the Heart

Pema Chödrön

SLOGANS TRANSLATED BY THE
Nālandā Translation Committee

SHAMBHALA
Boulder 2017

SHAMBHALA PUBLICATIONS, INC.
4720 Walnut Street
Boulder, Colorado 80301
www.shambhala.com

9 8 7 6 5 4 3 2 1

Printed in the United States of America

♾ This edition is printed on acid-free paper that meets the
American National Standards Institute Z39.48 Standard.
♻ Shambhala Publications makes every effort to print on recycled
paper. For more information please visit www.shambhala.com.
Distributed in the United States by Penguin Random House, LLC,
and in Canada by Random House of Canada Ltd

Designed by Liz Quan

CONTENTS

INTRODUCTION

Training in Loving-Kindness and Compassion

For many years, the fifty-nine slogans that are contained in this book have been the primary focus of my personal practice and teaching. These Tibetan Buddhist slogans (called *lojong*, or "mind-training" teachings) offer pithy, powerful reminders on how to awaken our hearts in the midst of day-to-day life, under any circumstances.

The *lojong* teachings presented in this book come from a classical Tibetan text called *The Root Text of the Seven Points of Training the Mind* by Chekawa Yeshe Dorje. When I first read these slogans, I was struck by their unusual message: we can use everything we encounter in our lives—pleasant or painful—to awaken genuine, uncontrived compassion.

The *lojong* teachings include a very supportive meditation practice called *tonglen* ("taking in and sending out"). This is a powerful practice designed to help ordinary people like ourselves connect with the openness and softness of our hearts. Included with this book is a downloadable audio program in which I offer in-depth instruction on *tonglen* practice. You can download the program at www.shambhala.com/openingtheheart.

The basic notion of *lojong* is that we can make friends with what we reject, what we see as "bad" in ourselves and in other people. At the same time, we could learn to be generous with what we cherish, what we see as "good." If we begin to live in this way, something in us that may have been buried for a long time begins to ripen. Traditionally, this "something" is called *bodhichitta*, or "awakened heart." It's something that we already have but usually have not yet discovered.

It's as if we were poor, homeless, hungry, and cold, and although we didn't know it, right under the ground where we always slept was a pot of gold. That gold is *bodhichitta*. Our confusion and misery come from not knowing that the gold is right here—and from always looking somewhere else. When we talk about joy, enlightenment, waking up, or awakening *bodhichitta*, all that means is that we know the gold is right here, and we realize that it's been here all along.

The basic message of the *lojong* teachings is that if it's painful, you can learn to hold your seat and move closer to that pain. Reverse the usual pattern, which is to split, to escape. Go against the grain and hold your seat. *Lojong* introduces a different attitude toward unwanted stuff: if it's painful, you become willing not just to endure it but also to let it awaken your heart and soften you. You learn to embrace it.

If an experience is delightful or pleasant, usually we want to grab it and make it last. We're afraid that it will end. We're not inclined to share it. The *lojong* teachings encourage us, if we enjoy what we are experiencing, to think of other people and wish for them to feel that. Share the wealth. Be generous with your joy. Give away what you most want. Be generous with your insights and delights. Instead of fearing that they're going to slip away and holding on to them, share them.

Whether it's pain or pleasure, through *lojong* practice we come to have a sense of letting our experience be as it is without trying to manipulate it, push it away, or grasp it. The pleasurable aspects of being human as well as the painful ones become the key to awakening *bodhichitta*.

Working with the *Lojong* Slogans

The method I suggest is one that was recommended to me by my teacher, Tibetan meditation master Chögyam Trungpa.

1. Each morning, pick a slogan at random from the book.
2. Read commentary on that slogan. (In addition to my own comments offered here, you could also consult additional commentaries on the *lojong* slogans. See the book list in the Additional Resources section for recommendations.)
3. Try to live by the meaning of that slogan throughout your day.

Sometimes, over the course of a day, I forget the slogan I've selected. Usually, however, if something challenging arises, the slogan of the day, or perhaps a different one altogether, will come to mind and provide me with valuable on-the-spot instruction. The slogans always introduce me to a bigger perspective, and I begin to gain confidence that I can use them to become less reactive and see things more clearly throughout my life. Even the most difficult of situations have become more and more workable.

I hope that slogan practice will help you, as it has helped me, to transform all circumstances into the path of enlightenment.

THE *LOJONG* SLOGANS
WITH COMMENTARY

First, train in the preliminaries.

The preliminaries are also known as the four reminders. In your daily life, try to:

1. Maintain an awareness of the preciousness of human life.

2. Be aware of the reality that life ends; death comes for everyone.

3. Recall that whatever you do, whether virtuous or not, has a result; what goes around comes around.

4. Contemplate that as long as you are too focused on self-importance and too caught up in thinking about how you are good or bad, you will suffer. Obsessing about getting what you want and avoiding what you don't want does not result in happiness.

2

Regard all dharmas as dreams.

COMMENTARY

Whatever you experience in your life—pain, pleasure, heat, cold, or anything else—is like something happening in a dream. Although you might think things are very solid, they are like passing memory. You can experience this open, unfixated quality in sitting meditation; all that arises in your mind—hate, love, and all the rest—is not solid. Although the experience can get extremely vivid, it is just a product of your mind. Nothing solid is really happening.

3

Examine the nature of unborn
awareness.

Look at your mind, at just simple awareness itself. "Examine" doesn't mean analyze. It means just looking and seeing if there is anything solid to hold on to. Our mind is constantly shifting and changing. Just look at that!

Self-liberate even the antidote.

Do not hang on to anything—even the realization that there's nothing solid to hold on to.

Rest in the nature of *alaya*,
the essence.

There is a resting place, a starting place that you can always return to. You can always bring your mind back home and rest right here, right now, in present, unbiased awareness.

In postmeditation,
be a child of illusion.

When you finish sitting meditation, if things become heavy and solid, be fully present and realize that everything is actually pliable, open, and workable. This is instruction for meditation in action, realizing that you don't have to feel claustrophobic because there is always lots of room, lots of space.

Sending and taking should be
practiced alternately.
These two should ride the breath.

This is instruction for a meditation practice called *tonglen*. In this practice you send out happiness to others and you take in any suffering that others feel. You take in with a sense of openness and compassion and you send out in the same spirit. People need help, and with this practice we extend ourselves to them.

Three objects, three poisons,
and three seeds of virtue.

The three objects are: friends, enemies, and neutrals. The three poisons are: craving, aversion, and indifference. When you feel craving, you own it fully and wish that all beings could be free of it. When you feel aggression or indifference you do the same. In this way what usually causes suffering—what poisons us and others—becomes a seed of compassion and loving-kindness, a seed of virtue.

In all activities, train with slogans.

Recalling any of these slogans "on the spot" can dissolve our self-centeredness and unkindness.

Begin the sequence of sending and taking with yourself.

Whatever pain you feel, take it in, wishing for all beings to be free of it. Whatever pleasure you feel, send it out to others. In this way, our personal problems and delights become a stepping-stone for understanding the suffering and happiness of all beings.

When the world is filled with evil,
Transform all mishaps into
the path of *bodhi*.

Whatever problems occur in your life, instead of reacting to them in the usual habitual way, you could transform them into the path of the *bodhi* heart. That is to say, you could awaken your compassionate and open heart. Use the *tonglen* approach and breathe in the pain of the situation, wishing that all beings could be free of it. Then breathe out and send loving-kindness to all suffering beings, including yourself!

12

Drive all blames into one.

This is advice on how to work with your fellow beings. Everyone is looking for someone to blame and therefore aggression and neurosis keep expanding. Instead, pause and look at what's happening with *you*. When you hold on so tightly to your view of what *they* did, you get hooked. Your own self-righteousness causes you to get all worked up and to suffer. So work on cooling that reactivity rather than escalating it. This approach reduces suffering—yours and everyone else's.

Be grateful to everyone.

Others will always show you exactly where you are stuck. They say or do something and you automatically get hooked into a familiar way of reacting—shutting down, speeding up, or getting all worked up. When you react in the habitual way, with anger, greed, and so forth, it gives you a chance to see your patterns and work with them honestly and compassionately. Without others provoking you, you remain ignorant of your painful habits and cannot train in transforming them into the path of awakening.

14

Seeing confusion as the four kayas
Is unsurpassable *shunyata* protection.

COMMENTARY

Through meditation practice you begin to realize that:

1. Your thoughts have no birthplace, they just pop up out of nowhere—that is called *dharmakaya*.

2. Thoughts are nevertheless unceasing—this is *sambhogakaya*.

3. They appear but are not solid—that is *nirmanakaya*.

4. Putting that all together, there is no birth, no dwelling, no cessation—this is *svabhavikakaya*.

This understanding gives the unsurpassable protection of realizing what is called *shunyata*, or "complete openness." There's nothing solid to react to. You have made much ado about nothing!

Four practices are the best of methods.

COMMENTARY

The four practices are:

1. *accumulating merit* through any actions or words that lessen self-absorption and thus create more space in your mind and heart,

2. *laying down evil deeds* through honest and joyful self-reflection,

3. *offering to the döns** by welcoming mishaps because they wake you up, and

4. *offering to the dharmapalas†* by expressing your gratitude to those who protect the teachings that help you and your fellow beings to wake up.

* Traditionally, a *dön* is a malevolent spirit, but it was explained by my teacher Chögyam Trungpa Rinpoche as a sudden wake-up call. Everything is going smoothly and suddenly something shocking happens.

† The *dharmapalas* are the protectors. They represent our basic awareness and manifest as outer situations that bring us back when we stray into unkindness and confusion of all kinds.

Whatever you meet unexpectedly,
join with meditation.

The unexpected will stop your mind. Rest in that space. When thoughts start again, do *tonglen*, breathing in whatever pain you may feel, thinking that others also feel like this, and gradually becoming more and more willing to feel this pain with the wish that others won't have to suffer. If it is a "good" shock, send out any joy you may feel, wishing for others to feel it also. Meeting the unexpected is also an opportunity to practice patience and nonaggression.

Practice the five strengths,
The condensed heart instructions.

The five strengths are:

1. *strong determination* to train in opening the heart and mind;

2. *familiarization* with the practices (such as *tonglen*) that help you to do that;

3. the *positive seed* that is within you, experienced as a yearning to practice and wake up;

4. *reproach*, which is a tricky one for Western students but is an important practice: realizing that ego-clinging causes you to suffer, you delight in self-reflection, in honesty, and in seeing where you get stuck; and

5. the *aspiration* to help alleviate suffering in this world, expressing that intention to yourself.

The mahayana instruction for the
ejection of consciousness at death
Is the five strengths: how you
conduct yourself is important.

COMMENTARY

When you are dying, practice the five strengths (based on becoming very familiar with them while you are alive).

1. *Strong determination:* Open and let go when the appearances of this world start to dissolve.

2. *Familiarization:* Practice opening and letting go throughout your life so you will not panic as everything dissolves at death.

3. *The positive seed:* Trust that you have the innate ability to let go and to feel compassion for others.

4. *Reproach:* Realizing that this limited identity isn't solid and is dissolving, do not indulge in trying to keep it from falling apart.

5. *Aspiration:* At death, aspire to spend all your future lives in the presence of your teachers and to do your best to benefit others forever.

All dharma agrees at one point.

The entire Buddhist teachings (dharma) are about lessening one's self-absorption, one's ego-clinging. This is what brings happiness to you and all beings.

20

Of the two witnesses,
hold the principal one.

The two witnesses of what you do are others and yourself. Of these two, you are the only one who really knows exactly what is going on. So work with seeing yourself with compassion but without any self-deception.

Always maintain only a joyful mind.

Constantly apply cheerfulness, if for no other reason than because you are on this spiritual path. Have a sense of gratitude to everything, even difficult emotions, because of their potential to wake you up.

If you can practice even
when distracted, you are well trained.

If you are a good horseback rider, your mind can wander but you don't fall off your horse. In the same way, whatever circumstances you encounter, if you are well trained in meditation, you don't get swept away by emotions. Instead they perk you up and your awareness increases.

Always abide by the three
basic principles.

COMMENTARY

The three basic principles are:

1. *Keeping the promises you made* if you took refuge vows and bodhisattva vows. When we take the refuge vow, we vow to take refuge in the Buddha, as an example of how to open and let go, the dharma (Buddha's teachings) as instructions on how to do this, and the sangha, the community of those who are also on this path. When we take the bodhisattva vow, we vow to awaken in order to help others to do the same.

2. *Refraining from outrageous conduct* or not engaging in what is sometimes called "bodhisattva exhibitionism."

3. *Developing patience* in both difficult an delightful situations.

Change your attitude,
but remain natural.

COMMENTARY

Work on reversing your caught-up, self-important
attitude and remain relaxed in this process.
Instead of always being caught in a prison of self-
absorption, look out and express gentleness to all
things. Then just relax.

Don't talk about injured limbs.

Don't try to build yourself up by talking about other people's defects.

Don't ponder others.

Don't ponder others' weak points, becoming arrogant about your own accomplishments.

27

Work with the greatest defilements
first.

Gain insight into your greatest obstacles—pride, aggression, self-denigration, and so forth—and work with those first. Do this with clarity and compassion.

Abandon any hope of fruition.

The key instruction is to stay in the present.
Don't get caught up in hopes of what you'll achieve
and how good your situation will be some day in
the future. What you do right now is what matters.

29

Abandon poisonous food.

You can use these slogans to build up your ego.
For instance, you refrain from talking about others'
defects or maligning them but only so people will
praise you. In this way, compassionate teachings
designed to lessen your sense of self-centeredness
become like rotten food that poisons you and
deceives others.

Don't be so predictable.

Do not hold a grudge against those who have done you wrong.

31

Don't malign others.

You speak badly of others, thinking it will make you feel superior. This only sows seeds of meanness in your heart, causing others not to trust you and causing you to suffer.

32

Don't wait in ambush.

Don't wait for the moment when someone you
don't like is weak to let them have it. This may
bring immediate satisfaction, but in the long run
it poisons you.

33

Don't bring things to a painful point.

Don't humiliate people.

Don't transfer the ox's load to the cow.

Don't transfer your load to someone else. Take responsibility for what is yours.

Don't try to be the fastest.

Don't compete with others.

36

Don't act with a twist.

Acting with a twist means having an ulterior motive
of benefiting yourself. It's the sneaky approach.
For instance, in order to get what you want for
yourself, you may temporarily take the blame for
something or help someone out.

Don't make gods into demons.

Don't use these teachings and practices to
strengthen your self-absorption.

Don't seek others' pain as the limbs
of your own happiness.

Don't build your happiness on the suffering of others.

39

All activities should be done
with one intention.

Whatever you are doing, take the attitude of
wanting it directly or indirectly to benefit others.
Take the attitude of wanting it to increase your
experience of kinship with your fellow beings.

Correct all wrongs with one intention.

"Wrongs" here refers to difficult circumstances
that we encounter. Our intention is to use these
situations to develop compassion for all the beings
who also suffer from difficulties and to aspire to
breathe in their pain with the practice of *tonglen*.

41

Two activities: one at the beginning,
one at the end.

In the morning when you wake up, you reflect on the day ahead and aspire to use it to keep a wide-open heart and mind. At the end of the day, before going to sleep, you think over what you have done. If you fulfilled your aspiration, even once, rejoice in that. If you went against your aspiration, rejoice that you are able to see what you did and are no longer living in ignorance. This way you will be inspired to go forward with increasing clarity, confidence, and compassion in the days that follow.

Whichever of the two occurs,
be patient.

Whatever happens in your life, joyful or painful, do not be swept away by reactivity. Be patient with yourself and don't lose your sense of perspective.

Observe these two,
even at the risk of your life.

The "two" referred to here are:

1. your refuge vows (to take refuge in that which
   is not based on ego-gratification but on the open,
   unbiased nature of the Buddha, the dharma, and
   the sangha) and

2. your bodhisattva vows (to use your life to awaken
   in order to help all beings to do the same).

Train in the three difficulties.

The three difficulties (or the three difficult practices) are:

1. to recognize your neurosis as neurosis,

2. then to *not* do the habitual thing, but to do something different to interrupt the neurotic habit, and

3. to make this practice a way of life.

Take on the three principal causes.

COMMENTARY

The three principal causes that allow us to put these teachings into practice are: a qualified teacher, a mind that turns toward awakening, and supportive circumstances.

46

Pay heed that the three never wane.

The "three" referred to here are: gratitude toward one's teacher, appreciation of the teachings, and conduct that is based on your refuge and bodhisattva vows. With the refuge vow, one takes refuge in the Buddha as an example, the dharma (Buddha's teachings) as instruction, and the sangha as the community of practitioners who wholeheartedly follow these instructions. With the bodhisattva vow, one aspires to use one's life to awaken in order to help all beings to do the same.

47

Keep the three inseparable.

The "three" referred to here are your body, speech, and mind. Your actions, speech, and thoughts should be inseparable from your mind training (training your mind in compassion and wisdom).

Train without bias in all areas.
It is crucial always to do this
pervasively and wholeheartedly.

It is important to include everyone and everything that you meet as part of your practice. They become the means by which you cultivate compassion and wisdom.

49

Always meditate on whatever
provokes resentment.

Do *tonglen* practice whenever you feel resentment. Do it with small things all the time. Then you will be prepared to work with the big ones when they arise.

50

Don't be swayed by external
circumstances.

Whether you are sick or well, rich or poor, comfortable or uncomfortable, practice *tonglen*. Whatever is wanted, send that out for others to enjoy. Whatever is unwanted, breathe that in, experiencing it directly for yourself and all the others who are in the same boat.

This time, practice the main points.

In this very life do not waste the opportunity to practice the main points:

1. Seeking to help others is more important than only looking out for yourself.

2. Practicing what your teacher has taught you is more important than scholarly study.

3. Awakening compassion (and thus lessening selfishness) is more important than any other spiritual practice.

Don't misinterpret.

COMMENTARY

There are six teachings that you might misinterpret: patience, yearning, excitement, compassion, priorities, and joy. The misinterpretations are:

1. You're patient when it means you'll get your way but not when your practice brings up challenges.

2. You yearn for worldly things but not for an open heart and mind.

3. You get excited about wealth and entertainment but not about your potential for enlightenment.

4. You have compassion for those you like and admire but not for those you don't.

5. Worldly gain is your priority rather than cultivating loving-kindness and compassion.

6. You feel joy when your enemies suffer, but you do not rejoice in others' good fortune.

Don't vacillate.

If you train in awakening compassion only some of the time, it will slow down the process of giving birth to certainty. Wholeheartedly train in keeping your heart and mind open to everyone.

54

Train wholeheartedly.

Train enthusiastically in strengthening your natural capacity for compassion and loving-kindness.

Liberate yourself by examining
and analyzing.

COMMENTARY

Know your own mind with honesty and
fearlessness. See what leads to more freedom and
what leads to more suffering. This can liberate
you from continually getting hooked by self-
centered thoughts and emotions, the root of all
dissatisfaction.

56

Don't wallow in self-pity.

Catch yourself when you do this and recognize that it just increases your suffering (and that of others).

Don't be jealous.

Work with jealousy when it's small, otherwise when it hits full force, you'll be swept away.

58

Don't be frivolous.

Don't waste your precious time. You never know
how long you have.

Don't expect applause.

Don't count on receiving credit for your good deeds.
Just do them anyway!

ADDITIONAL RESOURCES

Books about *Lojong* from Shambhala Publications

Chödrön, Pema. *Start Where You Are: A Guide to Compassionate Living.* Boston. In this book I offer longer commentaries on each slogan, along with instruction in *tonglen* and basic sitting meditation. (Use the alphabetical index of slogans at the end of the book to find the slogan you're working with.)

Kongtrül, Jamgön. *The Great Path of Awakening.* Translated by Ken McLeod. This is a translation of *The Seven Points of Mind Training* featuring the commentary of Jamgön Kongtrül, a renowned nineteenth-century master of Tibetan Buddhism.

Trungpa, Chögyam. *Training the Mind and Cultivating Loving-Kindness.* In this book Tibetan meditation master Chögyam Trungpa presents the practice of *lojong* to Westerners, offering wonderful commentary on each slogan and showing us how this practice can help us to overcome fear and self-centeredness.

Audio and Video

Audio and video recordings of talks and seminars by Pema Chödrön are available from:

The Pema Chödrön Foundation
(607) 738-5232
www.pemachodronfoundation.org

Sounds True
(800) 333-9185
www.soundstrue.com

Kalapa Recordings
(888) 450-1002
www.shambhalashop.com

Practice Centers

For information about meditation instruction or to find a practice center near you, please contact:

Shambhala International
1084 Tower Road
Halifax, NS B3H 2Y5
Canada
(902) 420-1118
www.shambhala.org

INDEX OF SLOGANS

LIBRARY OF CONGRESS CATALOGING-IN-PUBLICATION DATA

Names: Chödrön, Pema, author.

Title: The compassion book: teachings for awakening the heart / Pema Chödrön.

Other titles: Always maintain a joyful mind

Description: Boulder: Shambhala, 2017.

Identifiers: LCCN 2016029890 | ISBN 9781611804201 (paperback: alk. paper)

Subjects: LCSH: Ye-shes-rdo-rje, Chad-kha-ba, 1102-1176. Blo sbyong don bdun ma. | Blo-sbyong. | Spiritual life--Buddhism. | BISAC: RELIGION / Buddhism General (see also PHILOSOPHY / Buddhist). | BODY, MIND & SPIRIT / Meditation. | SELF-HELP / Meditations.

Classification: LCC BQ7805 .C484 2017 | DDC 294.3/444—dc23

LC record available at https://lccn.loc.gov/2016029890

HEART ADVICE

Weekly Quotes from Pema Chödrön

Visit shambhala.com/pemaheartadvice to sign up for Heart Advice and receive weekly words of wisdom from Pema Chödrön.